10 Techniques for Crafting Better Ads

10 Techniques for Crafting Better Ads

"The difference is only in degree. Advertising is multiplied salesmanship. It may appeal to thousands while the salesman talks to one. It involves a corresponding cost. Some people spend $10 per word on an average advertisement. Therefore every ad should be a super-salesman.

"A salesman's mistake may cost little. An advertiser's mistake may cost a thousand times that much. Be more cautious, more exacting, therefore. A mediocre salesman may affect a small part of your trade. Mediocre advertising affects all of your trade."

These points are as true today as they were when they were written nearly one hundred years ago!

So the goal then becomes: **how can we make our advertising as effective as possible.**

The answer is to test. Test again. And then test some more.

If ad "A" receives a two percent response rate, and ad "B" receives three percent, then we can deduce that ad "B" will continue to outperform ad "A" on a larger scale.

Testing takes time, however, and can be expensive if not kept in check. Therefore, it's ideal to start with some proven tested known ideas and work from there.

For example, if testing has shown for decades or more that targeted advertising significantly outperforms untargeted advertising (and it does), then we can start with that assumption and go from there.

If we know based on test results that crafting an ad that speaks directly to an individual performs better than addressing the masses (again, it does), then it makes little sense to start testing with the assumption that it does not. This is common sense.

So it stands to reason that knowing some basic rules or techniques about writing effective copy is in order. Test results will always trump everything, but it's better to have a starting point before you test.

So this starting point is the essence of this book.

The ten tips expressed here have been generally time-tested and known to be effective.

But I can't emphasize enough that when using these techniques, you should always test them before rolling out a large (and expensive) campaign.

Sometimes a little tweak here or there is all that is needed to increase response rates dramatically.

And with that, let's move onward...

Focus on Them, Not You

When a prospect reads your ad, letter, brochure, etc., the one thing he will be wondering from the start is: "what's in it for me?"

And if your copy doesn't tell him, it'll land in the trash faster than he can read the headline or lead.

A lot of advertisers make this mistake. They focus on them as a company. How long they've been in business, who their biggest customers are, how they've spent ten years of research and millions of dollars on developing this product, blah, blah.

Actually, those points are important. But they should be expressed in a way that matters to your potential customer. Remember, once he's thrown it in the garbage, the sale is lost!

When writing your copy, it helps to think of it as writing a letter to an old friend. In fact, I often picture a friend of mine who most closely fits my prospect's profile. What would I say to convince this friend to try my product? How would I target my friend's objections and beliefs to help *my cause?*

When you're writing to a friend, you'll use the pronouns "I" and "you." When trying to convince your friend, you might say: "Look, I know you think you've tried every widget out there. But you should know that..."

And it goes beyond just writing in the second person. That is, addressing your prospect as "you" within the copy. The fact of the matter is there are many successful ads that *weren't* written in the second person. Some are written in the first person perspective, where the writer uses "I." Other times the third person is used, with "she," "he," and "them."

And even if you *do* write in the second person, it doesn't necessarily mean your copy is about them.

For example:

> "As a real estate agent, you can take comfort in the fact that I've sold over 10,000 homes and mastered the tricks of the trade"

Although you're writing in the second person, you're really still focusing on yourself.

So how *can* you focus on them? Glad you asked. One way is to...

Emphasize Benefits, Not Features

What are features? They are descriptions of what qualities a product possesses.

- The XYZ car delivers 55 miles per gallon in the city.
- Our ladder's frame is made from a lightweight durable steel alloy.
- Our glue is protected by a patent.
- This database has a built-in data-mining system.

And what are benefits? They are what those features mean to your prospects.

- You'll save money on gas *and* cut down on environmental pollutants when you use our energy saving high-performance hybrid car. Plus, you'll feel the extra *oomph* when you're passing cars, courtesy of the efficient electric motor, which <u>they don't have</u>!
- Lightweight durable steel-alloy frame means you'll be able to take it with you with ease, and use it in places most other ladders can't go, while still supporting up to 800 pounds. No more backaches lugging around that heavy ladder. And it'll last for 150 years, so you'll never need to buy another ladder again!
- Patent-protected glue ensures you can use it on wood, plastic, metal, ceramic, glass, and tile...without messy cleanup and without ever having to re-glue it again—guaranteed!
- You can instantly see the "big picture" hidden in your data, *and* pull the most arcane statistics on demand. Watch your business do a "180" in no time flat, when you instantly know why it's failing in the first place! It's all done with our built-in data-mining system that's so easy to use, my twelve year-old son used it successfully *right out of the box*.

I just made up those examples, but I think you understand my point.

By the way, did you notice in the list of features where I wrote "steel alloy?" But in the benefits I wrote "steel-alloy" (with a hyphen). Not sure off-hand which one is correct, but I know which one I'd use.

Here's why: you are not writing to impress your English teacher or win any awards. The only award you're after is your copy beating the control (control being the best-selling copy so far), so take some liberty in grammar, punctuation, and sentence structure. You want it to be read and acted upon, not read and admired!

But—back to benefits…

If you were selling an expensive watch, you wouldn't tell your reader that the face is 2 inches in diameter and the band is made of leather.

You *show* him how the extra-large face will tell him the time at a glance. No sir! He won't have to squint and look foolish to everyone around him trying to read this magnificent timepiece. And how about the way he'll project success and charisma when he wears the beautiful gold watch with its handcrafted custom leather band? How his lover will find him irresistible when he's all dressed up to go out, wearing the watch. Or how the watch's status and beauty will attract the ladies.

Incidentally, did you notice how I brought up *not squinting* as a benefit? Does that sound like a silly benefit? Not if you are selling to affluent baby boomers suffering from degrading vision. They probably hate it when someone they're trying to impress sees them squint in order to read something. It's all part of their inner desire, which you need to discover. And which <u>even *they* may not know about</u>. That is, until you show them a better way.

The point is to address the benefits of the product, not its features. And when you do that, you're focusing on your reader and his interests, his desires. The trick is to highlight those specific benefits (and word them correctly) that push your reader's emotional hot buttons.

How do you do that? Read on!

Push Their Emotional Hot Buttons

This is where research really pays off. Because in order to push those buttons, you need to first know what they are.

Listen to this story first, and I'll tell you what I mean: Once upon a time a young man walked into a Chevrolet dealer's showroom to check out a Chevy Camaro. He had the money, and he was ready to make a buying decision. But he couldn't decide if he wanted to buy the Camaro or the Ford Mustang up the road at the Ford dealer.

A salesman approached him and soon discovered the man's dilemma.

"Tell me what you like best about the Camaro," said the salesman.

"It's a <u>fast</u> car. I like it for its speed."

After some more discussion, the salesman learned the man had just started dating a cute college cheerleader. So what did the salesman do?

Simple. He changed his pitch accordingly, to push the hot buttons he knew would help advance the sale. He told the man about how impressed his new girlfriend would be <u>*when he came home with this car!*</u> He placed the mental image in the man's mind of he and his girlfriend cruising to the beach in the Camaro. How all of his friends will be envious when they see him riding around with a beautiful girl in a beautiful car.

And suddenly the man saw it. He got it. And the salesman recognized this and piled it on even more. Before you know it, the man wrote a nice fat check to the Chevy dealership, because he was *sold!*

The salesman found those hot buttons and pushed them like never before until the man realized he wanted the Camaro more than he wanted his money.

I know what you're thinking...the man said he liked the car because it was fast, didn't he?

Yes, he did. But subconsciously, what he really desired was a car that would impress his girlfriend, his friends, and in his mind make them love him more! In his mind he equated speed with thrill. Not because he wanted an endless supply of speeding tickets, but because he thought that thrill would make him more attractive, more likeable.

Perhaps the man didn't even realize this fact himself. But the salesman sure did. And he knew which emotional hot buttons to press to get the sale.

Now, where does the research pay off?

Well, a good salesman knows how to ask the kinds of questions that will tell him which buttons to press on the fly. When you're writing copy, you don't have that luxury. It's therefore very important to know upfront the wants, needs, and desires of your prospects for that very reason. If you haven't done your homework, your prospect is going to decide that he'd rather keep his money than buy your product. Remember, copywriting is **salesmanship in print!**

It's been said many times: People don't like to be sold.

But they do like to buy.

And they buy based on emotion first and foremost. Then they justify their decision with logic, *even after they are already sold emotionally*. So be sure to back up your emotional pitch with logic to nurture that justification at the end.

And while we're on the subject, let's talk a moment about perceived "hype" in a sales letter. A lot of more "conservative" advertisers have decided that they don't like hype, because they consider hype to be old news, been-there-and-done-that, my customers won't fall for hype, it's not believable anymore.

What they should realize is that hype itself does not sell well. Some less experienced copywriters often try to compensate for their lack of research or not fully understanding their target market or the product itself by adding tons of adjectives and adverbs and exclamation points and big bold type.

Whew! If you do your job right, it's just not needed.

That's not to say some adverbs or adjectives don't have their place...only if they're used sparingly, and only if they _advance the sale_.

But I think you'd agree that backing up your copy with proof and believability will go a lot farther in convincing your prospects than "power words" alone. I say _power words_, because there are certain adverbs and adjectives that _have_ been proven to make a difference when they're included. This by itself is not hype. But repeated too often, they become less effective, and they take away (at least in your prospect's mind) from the proof.

Which brings us into our next tip...

Incorporating Proof and Believability

When your prospect reads your ad, you want to make sure he believes any claims you make about your product or service. Because if there's any doubt in his mind, he won't bite, no matter how sweet the deal. In fact, the "too good to be true" mentality will virtually guarantee a lost sale...even if it _is_ all true.

So what can you do to increase the _perception_ of believability? Because after all, it's the perception you need to address up front. But of course you also must make sure your copy is accurate and truthful.

Here are some tried and tested methods that will help:

- If you're dealing with existing customers who already know you deliver as promised, emphasize that trust. Don't leave it up to them to figure it out. Make them stop, cock their heads, and say, "Oh, yeah. The ABC Company _has_ never done me wrong before. I can trust them."

- Include testimonials of satisfied customers. Be sure to put full names and locations, where possible. Remember, "A.S." is a lot less believable than "Andy Sherman, Voorhees, NJ." If you can also include a picture of the customer and/or a professional title, that's even better. It doesn't matter that your testimonials aren't from somebody famous or that your prospect does not know these people personally. If you have enough compelling testimonials, and they're believable, you're much better off than not including them at all.

- Pepper your copy with facts and research findings to support your claims. Be sure to credit all sources, even if the fact is common knowledge, because a neutral source goes a long way towards credibility.

- For a direct mail letter or certain space ads where the copy is in the form of a letter from a specific individual, including a picture of that person helps. But unlike "traditional" real estate letters and other similar ads, I'd put the picture at the end near your signature, or midway through the copy, rather than at the top where it will detract from your headline. And...if your sales letter *is* from a specific individual, be sure to include his credentials to establish him as an expert in his field (relating to your product or service, of course).

- If applicable, cite any awards or third-party reviews the product or service has received.

- If you've sold a lot of widgets, tell them. It's the old "10 million people can't be wrong" adage (they can be, but your prospect will likely take your side on the matter).

- Include a GREAT return policy and *stand by it!* This is just good business policy. Many times, offering a double refund guarantee for certain products will result in higher profits. Yes, you'll dish out more refunds, but if you sell three times as many widgets as before, and only have to refund twice as much as before, it may be worth it, depending on your offer and return on investment. Crunch the numbers and see what makes sense. More importantly, *test!* Make them think, "Gee, they wouldn't be so generous with returns if they didn't stand behind their product!"

- If you can swing it, adding a celebrity endorsement will always help to establish credibility. Heck, if 'ol honest Abe Lincoln recommended your product and backs up your claims, it must be true! Ok, you get the idea, though.

- When it makes sense, use 3rd party testimonials. What are 3rd party testimonials? Here's some examples from some Web site copy I wrote when there weren't many customer testimonials available yet:

> **"Spyware, without question, is on an exponential rise over the last six months."**
> - Alfred Huger, Senior Director of Engineering, Symantec Security Response (maker of Norton security software)
>
> **"Simply clicking on a banner ad can install spyware."**
> - Dave Methvin, Chief Technology Officer, PC Pitstop
>
> **A deployment method is to "trick users into consenting to a software download they think they absolutely need"**
> - Paul Bryan, Director, Security And Technology Unit, Microsoft

Do you see what I did?

I took quotes from experts in their respective fields and turned them to my side. But...be sure to get their consent or permission from the copyright holder if there's ever any question about copyrighted materials as your source.

Note that I also pushed an emotional hot button: fear.

<u>It's been proven that people will generally do more to avoid pain than to obtain pleasure</u>. So why not use that tidbit of info to your advantage?

- Reveal a flaw about your product. This helps alleviate the "too good to be true" syndrome. You reveal a flaw that isn't really a flaw. Or reveal a flaw that is minor, just to show that you're being "up front" about your product's shortcomings.

    Example:

    "You're probably thinking right now that this tennis racket is a miracle worker—and it is. But I must tell you that it has one little...shortcoming.

    My racket takes about 2 weeks to get used to. In fact, when you first start using it, your game will actually get <u>worse</u>. But if you can just ride it out, you'll see a tremendous improvement in your volleys, net play, serves, ..." **And so on.**

    There's a tendency to think, with all of the ads that we are bombarded with today that every advertiser is always putting his best foot forward, so to speak. And I think that line of reasoning is accurate, to a point.

    But isn't it refreshing when someone stands out from the crowd and is honest? In other words, your reader will start to subconsciously believe that you are revealing all of the flaws, even though your best foot *still* stands forward.

- Use "lift notes." These are a brief note or letter from a person of authority. Not necessary a celebrity, although that can add credibility, too. A person of authority is someone well recognized in their field (which is related to your product) that they are qualified to talk about. Lift notes may be distributed as inserts, a separate page altogether, or even as part of the copy itself. As always, *test!*

- If you are limiting the offer with a deadline "order by" date, be sure the deadline is real and does not change. Deadline dates that change every day are sure to reduce credibility. The prospect will suspect, "if his deadline date keeps changing, he's not telling the truth about it...I wonder what else he's not telling the truth about."

- Avoid baseless "hype." I discussed that in my previous tip. Enough said.

The Unique Selling Proposition (USP)

Also known as the unique selling *position*, the USP is often one of the most oft-misunderstood elements of a good sales letter. It's what separates your product or service from your competitors. Let's take a quick look at some unique selling propositions for a product itself:

1) **Lowest Price** – If you've got the corner marketed on budget prices, flaunt it. Walmart has made this USP famous lately, but it's not new to them. In fact, selling for cheaper has been around as long as capitalism itself. Personally, I'm not crazy about price wars, because someone can always come along and sell for cheaper. Then it's time for a new strategy...

2) **Superior Quality** – If it outperforms your competitor's product or is made with higher quality materials, it's a good bet that you could use this fact to your advantage. For example, compare Breyers Ice Cream to their competitor's. From the packaging to the wholesome superior ingredients, the quality is evident. It may cost a little more than their competitor's ice cream, but for their market, it sells.

3) **Superior Service** – If you offer superior service over your competitor's, people will buy from you instead. This is

especially true with certain markets that are all about service: long-distance, Internet service providers, cable television, etc.

4) **Exclusive Rights** – My favorite! If you can legitimately claim that your product is protected by a patent or copyright, licensing agreement, etc., then you have a winner for exclusive rights. If you have a patent, even the *President of the U.S.* must buy it from you.

Ok, what if your product or service is no different than your competitor's? I would disagree, because there are always differences. The trick is to turn them into a positive advantage for you. You want to put your "best foot forward." So what can we do in this scenario?

One way is to present something that your company has devised internally that no other company does. Look, there's a reason why computer store "A" offers to beat their competitor's price for the same product by X%. If you look closely, the two packages are never exactly the same. Company "B" offers a free scanner, while company "A" offers a free printer. Or some other difference. They are comparing apples to oranges. So unless you find a company with the exact same package (you won't...they've seen to that), you won't be able to cash in.

But what if you truly have the same widget for sale as the guy up the road?

Unless your prospect knows the inner workings of both your and your competitor's product, including the manufacturing process, customer service, and everything in-between, then you have a little potential creative licensing here. But you must be truthful.

For example, if I tell my readers that my product is bathed in steam to ensure purity and cleanliness (like the cans and bottles in most beer manufacturing processes), it doesn't matter that Joe's Beer up the road does the same thing. That fact that Joe doesn't advertise this fact makes it a USP in your prospect's eyes.

Want some more USP examples?

- We are the only car repair shop that will *buy your car* if you are not 100 percent satisfied with our work.

- Delivered in 30 minutes or it's on us!

- No other furniture company will pay for your shipping.

- Our recipe is so secret, only three people in the world know it!

As with most ways to boost copy response, research is the key with your USP. Sometimes your USP is obvious, for example if you have a patent. Other times you must do a little legwork to discover it (or shape it to your target market).

Here's where a little persistence and in-person selling really pays off. Let me give you an example to illustrate what I mean:

Suppose your company sells beanbag chairs for kids. So you, being the wise marketer that you are, decide to sell these beanbags in person to prospects before writing your copy. After completing twenty different pitches for your product, you discover that 75 percent of those you visited asked if the chair would eventually leak. Since the chairs are for kids, it's only logical that parents would be concerned about their youngster jumping on it, rolling on it, and doing all things possible to break the seam and "spill the beans."

So when you write your copy, you make sure you address that issue: "You can rest assure that our super-strong beanbag chairs are triple-stitched for guaranteed leak-proof performance. No other company will make this guarantee about their beanbag chairs!"

The Headline

If you're going to make a single change to boost your response rate the most, focus on your headline (you *do* have one, don't you?).

Why? Because <u>five times</u> as many people read your headline than your copy. Quite simply, a headline is...an ad for your ad. People won't stop their busy lives to read your copy unless you give them a good reason to do so. So a good headline promises some news and a benefit.

Perhaps you're thinking, "What's this about news, you say?"

Think about the last time you browsed through your local newspaper. You checked out the articles, one by one, and occasionally an ad may have caught your eye. Which ads were the ones most likely to catch your eye?

The ones that looked like an article, of course.

The ones with the headline that promised news.

The ones with fonts and type that closely resembled the fonts and type used in articles.

The ones that were placed where articles were placed (as opposed to being placed on a full page of ads, for example).

And the ones with the most compelling headlines that convinced you it's worth a few minutes to read the copy.

The headline is *that* powerful and *that* important.

I've seen many ads over the years that didn't even *have* a headline. And that's just silly. It's the equivalent of flushing good money spent on advertising right down the toilet.

Why? Because your response can increase dramatically by not only adding a headline, but by making that headline almost impossible to resist *for your target market.*

And those last three words are important. ***Your target market.***

For example, take a look at the following headline:

Announcing...New High-Tech Gloves Protect Wearer Against Hazardous Waste

News, <u>and</u> a benefit.

Will that headline appeal to everyone?

No, and you don't care about everyone.

But for someone who handles hazardous waste, they would sure appreciate knowing about this little gem.

That's your target market, and it's your job to get them to read your ad. Your headline is the way you do that.

Ok, now where do you find great headlines?

You look at other successful ads (especially direct response) that have stood the test of time. You look for ads that run regularly in magazines and other publications. How do you know they're good? Because if they didn't do their job, the advertiser wouldn't keep running them again and again.

You get on the mailing lists of the big direct response companies like Agora and Boardroom and save their direct mail packages.

You read the National Enquirer.

Huh? You heard that correctly.

The National Enquirer has some of the best headlines in the business.

Pick up a recent issue and you'll see what I mean. Ok, now how could you adapt some of those headlines to your own product or service?

Your headline should create a sense of urgency. It should be as specific as possible (i.e. say $1,007,274.23 instead of "a million dollars").

The headline appearance is also very important. Make sure the type used is bold and large, and different from the type used in the copy. Generally, longer headlines tend to out pull shorter ones, even when targeting more "conservative" prospects.

Some other sites online where you can get great headlines (from master copywriter John Carlton, no less) are:

- http://www.trsdirect.com/
- http://www.ohpdirect.com/product.php

On each page, click on the individual products in order to view the ads and headlines.

It should go without saying that when you use other successful headlines, you adapt them to your own product or service. Never copy a headline (or any other written copyrighted piece of work for that matter) word for word. Copywriters and ad agencies are notoriously famous for suing for plagiarism. And rightfully so.

The More You Tell, The More You Sell

The debate on using long copy versus short copy never seems to end. Usually it is a newcomer to copywriting who seems to think that long copy is boring and, well...long. "I would never read that much copy," they say.

The fact of the matter is that all things being equal, long copy will outperform short copy every time. And when I say long copy, I don't mean long and boring, or long and untargeted.

The person who says he would never read all that copy is making a big mistaking in copywriting: he is going with his gut reaction instead of relying on test results. He is thinking that he himself is the prospect. He's not. We're never our own prospects.

There have been many studies and split tests conducted on the long copy versus short copy debate. And the clear winner is always long copy. But that's targeted relevant long copy as opposed to untargeted boring long copy.

Some significant research has found that readership tends to fall off dramatically at around 300 words, but does not drop off again until around 3,000 words.

If I'm selling an expensive set of golf clubs and send my long copy to a person who's plays golf occasionally, or always wanted to try golf, I am sending my sales pitch to the wrong prospect. It is not targeted effectively. And so if a person who receives my long copy doesn't read past the 300th word, they weren't qualified for my offer in the first place.

It wouldn't have mattered whether they read up to the 100th word or 10,000th word. They still wouldn't have made a purchase.

However, if I sent my long copy to an avid die-hard golfer, who just recently purchased other expensive golf products through the mail, painting an irresistible offer, telling him how my clubs will knock 10 strokes off his game, he'll likely read every word. And if I've targeted my message correctly, he will buy.

Remember, if your prospect is 3000 miles away, it's not easy for him to ask you a question. You must anticipate and answer all of his questions and overcome all objections in your copy if you are to be successful.

And make sure you don't throw everything you can think of under the sun in there. You only need to include as much information as you need to make the sale...and not one word more.

If it takes a 10-page sales letter, so be it. If it takes a 16-page magalog, fine. But if the 10-page sales letter tests better than the 16-page magalog, then by all means go with the winner.

Does that mean every prospect must read every word of your copy before he will order your product? Of course not.

Some will read every word and then go back and reread it again. Some will read the headline and lead, then skim much of the body and land on the close. Some will scan the entire body, then go back and read it. All of those prospects may end up purchasing the offer, but they also all may have different styles of reading and skimming.

Which brings us to the next tip...

Write To Be Scanned

Your layout is very important in a sales letter, because you want your letter to look inviting, refreshing to the eyes. In short, you want your prospect to stop what he's doing and read your letter.

If he sees a letter with tiny margins, no indentations, no breaks in the text, no white space, and no subheads...if he sees a page of nothing but densely-packed words, do you think he'll be tempted to read it?

Not likely.

If you do have ample white space and generous margins, short sentences, short paragraphs, subheads, and an italicized or underlined word here and there for emphasis, it will certainly look more inviting to read.

When reading your letter, some prospects will start at the beginning and read word for word. Some will read the headline and maybe the lead, then read the "P.S." at the end of the letter and see who the letter is from, then start from the beginning.

And some folks will scan through your letter, noticing the various subheads strategically positioned by you throughout your letter, then decide if it's worth their time to read the entire thing. Some may never read the entire letter, but order anyways.

You must write for all of them. Interesting and compelling long copy for the studious reader, and short paragraphs and sentences, white space, and subheads for the skimmer.

Subheads are the smaller headlines sprinkled throughout your copy.

Like this.

When coming up with your headline, some of the headlines that didn't make the cut can make great subheads. A good subhead forces your prospect to keep reading, threading him along from start to finish throughout your copy, while also providing the glue necessary to keep skimmers skimming.

The Structure of AIDAS

There's a well-known structure in successful sales letters, described by the acronym *AIDA*.

AIDA stands for:

- Attention
- Interest
- Desire
- Action

First, you capture your prospect's attention. This is done with your headline and lead. If your ad fails to capture your prospect's attention, it fails completely. Your prospect doesn't read your stellar copy, and doesn't order your product or service.

Then you want to build a strong interest in your prospect. You want him to keep reading, because if he reads, he just might buy.

Next, you channel a desire. Having a targeted market for this is key, because you're not trying to create a desire where one did not already exist. You want to capitalize on an existing desire, which your prospect *may or may not know he already has.* And you want your prospect to experience that desire for your product or service.

Finally, you present a call to action. You want him to pick up the telephone, return the reply card, attend the sales presentation, order your product, whatever. You need to ask for the sale (or response, if that's the goal). You don't want to beat around the bush at this point. If your letter and AIDA structure is sound and persuasive, here's where you present the terms of your offer and urge the prospect to act now.

A lot has been written about the AIDA copywriting formula. I'd like to add one more letter to the acronym: S for Satisfy.

In the end, after the sale is made, you want to satisfy your prospect, who is now a customer. You want to deliver exactly what you promised (or even more), by the date you promised, in the manner you promised. In short, you want to give him every reason in the world to trust you the next time you sell him a back-end offer. And of course you'd rather he doesn't return the product (although if he does, you also execute your return policy *as promised*).

Either way, you want your customers to be satisfied. It will make you a lot more money in the long run.

Use Takeaway Selling to Increase the Urgency

When you limit the supply of a product or service in some way (i.e. takeaway selling), basic economics dictates that the demand will rise. In other words, people will generally respond better to an offer if they believe the offer is about to become unavailable or restricted in some way.

And of course, the opposite is also true. If a prospect knows your product will be around whenever he needs it, there's no need for him to act now. And when your ad is put aside by the prospect, the chance of closing the sale diminishes greatly.

It's your job, therefore, to get your prospect to buy, and buy now. Using scarcity to sell is a great way to accomplish that.

There are basically three types of takeaways:

1) Limiting the quantity
2) Limiting the time
3) Limiting the offer

In the first method, limiting the quantity, you are presenting a fixed number of widgets available for sale. After they're gone, that's it.

Some good ways to limit the quantity include:

- only so many units made or obtained
- selling off old stock to make room for new
- limited number of cosmetically-defected items, or a fire sale
- only a limited number being sold so as not to saturate the market
- etc.

In the second method, limiting the time, a deadline is added to the offer. It should be a realistic deadline, not one that changes all the time (especially on a website, where the deadline date always seems to be that very day at midnight...when you return the next day, the deadline date has mysteriously changed again to the new day). Deadlines that change decrease your credibility.

This approach works well when the offer or the price will change, or the product/service will become unavailable, after the deadline.

The third method, limiting the offer, is accomplished by limiting other parts of the offer, such as the guarantee, bonuses or premiums, the price, and so on.

When using takeaway selling, you must be sure to follow-through with your restrictions. If you say you only have 500 widgets to sell, then don't sell 501. If you say your offer will expire at the end of the month, make sure it does. Otherwise your credibility will take a hit. Prospects will remember the next time another offer from you makes its way into their hands.

Another important thing you should do is explain the reason why the offer is being restricted. Don't just say the price will be going up in three weeks, but decline to tell them why.

Here are some examples of good takeaway selling:

"*Unfortunately, I can only handle so many clients. Once my plate is full, I will be unable to accept any new business. So if you're serious about strengthening your investment strategies and creating more wealth than ever before, you should contact me ASAP.*"

"*Remember...you must act by [date] at midnight in order to get my 2 bonuses. These bonuses have been provided by [third-party company], and we have no control over their availability after that time.*"

"*We've obtained only 750 of these premiums from our vendor. Once they are gone, we won't be able to get any more until next year. And even then we can't guarantee the price will remain the same. In fact, because of the increasing demand, it's very likely the price could double or triple by then!*"

Remember when I said earlier that people buy based on emotions, then back up their decision to buy with logic? Well, by using takeaway selling, that restriction becomes part of that logic to buy and buy now.

Conclusion

Great copy is made, not born. It is derived from proven test results designed to do one thing and do it well: sell.

Effective advertising doesn't always use "grammatically correct" English. It uses short sentences, fragments. Like this.

It convinces you to buy, and buy now. Period.

It talks about benefits, not features. It sells on emotion and reinforces the decision to buy with logic.

It paints a compelling picture and irresistible offer that forces your prospect to act and act now! And if it doesn't, then you drop that ad like a hot potato and go with one that does.

Effective persuasion is like your top salesperson--the one who continues to break all your sales records year after year--on the job 24 x 7, multiplied by thousands or millions! Just imagine if that salesperson, the one with proven results, could be multiplied as much as you wanted.

Now that would be effective (and cost-efficient) marketing!

www.ingramcontent.com/pod-product-compliance
Lightning Source LLC
LaVergne TN
LVHW021055100526
838202LV00083B/6239